T0119519

# THE TRUE STORY *of*
# SAINT NICHOLAS

# THE TRUE STORY *of* SAINT NICHOLAS

REBECCA BENSON HASKELL

ILLUSTRATED BY
ELIZABETH DURHAM GOODHUE

*Alan C. Hood & Company, Inc.*
CHAMBERSBURG, PENNSYLVANIA

ISBN 978-0-911469-29-5

Published by Alan C. Hood & Co., Inc.
Chambersburg, PA 17201

www.hoodbooks.com

Copies of *The True Story of Saint Nicholas* may be
obtained by sending $20.00 per copy to:

Alan C. Hood & Co., Inc.
P.O. Box 775, Chambersburg, PA 17201

Price includes postage and handling.
Quantity discounts are available to dealers and non-profit organizations.
Write on letterhead for details.

Cover and text adapted from the original design of
Kohn-Cruikshank Inc. by James F. Brisson

10 9 8 7 6 5 4 3 2

*The True Story of Saint Nicholas*

IS DEDICATED TO THE MEMORY OF

ELIZABETH DURHAM GOODHUE

# FOREWORD

At Grace Episcopal Church in
Salem, Massachusetts, one day in the early
1960s, I heard other parents complaining
Christmas had become too commercial. "And
Santa Claus!" one of them said. "What does he
have to do with Christmas?"

"Don't you know," I answered, "that Saint
Nicholas was a bishop of the early church?"
Their faces fell. None of them knew anything
about Saint Nicholas. For the life of me, I don't
know how I knew, except that my parents had
taken me to Italy when I was a child, and in
Italy you can't miss Saint Nicholas.

I set out to learn more about this remarkable man and began collecting bits and pieces of his story. The result of my research is this little book. It was originally published in a private edition and sold at church fairs. It fell out of print, but occasionally friends commented on how much pleasure it gave them. Some returned to it every year at Christmas time. In one family, the child who had most recently learned to read had the honor of reading it aloud.

With the encouragement of friends, I am reissuing this book in my eighty-eighth year. It is dedicated to the memory of my dear friend Betsy Goodhue, without whose lovely illustrations it would never have been published.

*Rebecca Benson Haskell*
MARBLEHEAD, MASSACHUSETTS, 1997

# THE TRUE STORY *of*
# SAINT NICHOLAS

ALONG, LONG TIME AGO, about two hundred and sixty years after Jesus was born in Bethlehem, a boy named Nicholas was born in Patara, a seaport town on the Xanthus river in the province of Lycia in Asia Minor. Not many people had heard about Jesus Christ and the good news He had brought to the world, but Nicholas's father and mother had, so they were called Christians. Saint Paul had sailed from Patara many years before, so perhaps his teachings about Jesus had been remembered by the people of the town. Today we know Asia Minor as Turkey, but in Nicholas's day it was part of the Roman Empire.

The Roman Emperor Diocletian believed that Christians were bad people, so he often put them in prison or even had them killed.

Nicholas grew up to be a fine man whom everyone loved. His parents died when he was about twenty and left him a great deal of money. Nicholas was very generous and gave everything he had to the poor people.

The story is told that a friend of his had three daughters. In that country a girl could not marry unless she could bring her husband a dowry, which meant money or land or animals like goats, sheep, or cattle. Nicholas's friend had lost all his possessions and was afraid that his daughters would have to be sold as slaves. Nicholas decided to help them, but as he did not want to be thanked, he went late at night to the man's house and threw a bag of gold through an open window. How happy that family was the next day! The eldest daughter was able to be married.

The next year the second daughter fell in love, but again there was no money for her dowry. Nicholas came in the night and tossed in another bag of gold. Of course the family did not know whom to thank.

When the youngest daughter was old enough to marry, her father remembered the other gifts, so he tried to stay awake in case the stranger returned. Sure enough, Nicholas came after dark. His friend caught him and asked why he gave these presents secretly. Nicholas must have told him that Jesus had said that when you give away something, do it secretly, for God our Father, who knows all that you do, will reward you. Some people say that Nicholas put the money in stockings and dropped them down the chimney. Perhaps that is why we hang our stockings by the fireplace on Christmas Eve.

Nicholas decided that he would spend his life telling people about Jesus and His Church, so he went to live with a group of men who also loved God. He soon became their leader and was made the abbot of the Monastery of Holy Sion, near the city of Myra, the capital of Lycia, northwest of the island of Cyprus.

Once he went on a ship to the Holy Land, to see the country where Jesus had lived. The sea became very rough, and the wind blew wildly. The sailors were frightened, but Nicholas prayed that they might have a safe voyage. His prayer was answered, and even today, when sailors leave port in that part of

the world, their friends say to them,
"May Saint Nicholas hold the tiller!"
Nicholas worked very hard for the
church, and when still a young man
he was made Bishop of Myra. Most of
the pictures that we find show him as
an old man with white hair and beard,
wearing a red cloak and a bishop's mitre.
A mitre is a hat which rises in two
points, one in front and one in back.
These points are symbols of the tongues
of flame which appeared on the heads
of the Apostles of Jesus at Pentecost.
Nicholas is often shown carrying a staff
shaped like a shepherd's crook. This
means that he is a shepherd of the flock
of Christ.

The Emperor Diocletian put Bishop
Nicholas and his friends in prison
because they taught people about Jesus,
but when Constantine became Emperor
in 306, they were released and allowed
to return to their churches and mon-
asteries. In the year 325 there was a
great meeting of all the Christian leaders
in Nicea, east of Constantinople. It is
said that Bishop Nicholas went to this
meeting. It was there that the church-
men wrote a statement of what they
believed called the Nicene Creed, which
is still in use in Christian churches. It
is possible that Saint Nicholas helped to
write it!

Nicholas died on December 6, 345.

Because he had always been such a good
Christian, he was called a saint.  The
tomb where he was buried became
a shrine where people came to pray.
About two hundred years after Nicholas's
death, the Emperor Justinian built a
church in his honor in Constantinople.

In the eleventh century the city of Myra
was captured by the Saracens, who
worshiped Mohammed and hated the
Christians.  Fearing that the Saracens
might destroy the body of the saint,
some Christians removed it from Myra
in 1087 and took it by boat to the city
of Bari in Italy.  For this reason Saint
Nicholas is sometimes called Nicholas
of Bari.

All through the years people told their
children about Saint Nicholas, and
he became the patron saint or special
guardian of young people (the story
of the three daughters); of sailors
(the story of his voyage); of prisoners
(he had been one); of travelers, bakers,
and many others.

December 6 is known as his feast day.
In many countries in Europe Saint
Nicholas is said to come and talk with
children on the eve of that day and
to ask whether they have been good.
Before they go to sleep children put
their shoes outside, sometimes filled
with candy for the saint or with hay for
his horse or reindeer.  The next morning

they awake to find the shoes full of toys and other presents. In these countries Christmas is celebrated as a church day.

The English Pilgrims and Puritans who first came to America did not believe that people should celebrate holy days or have parties. They thought people were good Christians only if they sat in church and listened to long talks about how bad they were! However, when the Dutch came and settled New Amsterdam, which is now New York, they brought with them the story of Sinterklaas (a short way of saying Sint Nicolaas). His feast day was forgotten here, but not the example which he set in giving presents secretly.

# AFTERWORD

IN 1822 a scholar named Clement Moore
wrote a poem for his children. It begins:
"'Twas the night before Christmas, when
all through the house / Not a creature
was stirring not even a mouse." Do you
know that the name of this poem is "A
Visit from Saint Nicholas"? When you
read it again this year, remember that the
"jolly old elf" called Saint Nick or Santa
Claus was once a real person who knew
that the greatest present in the world was
God's gift to us, the Baby Jesus who was
born in a manger on Christmas morning.

# ABOUT THE AUTHOR

REBECCA BENSON HASKELL was born in
Salem, Massachusetts, in 1909, and graduated from
Concord Academy at the age of sixteen. She was
the first women on the board of directors of Salem
Hospital. Mrs. Haskell had two children, four
grandchildren, and two great-grandchildren. After
living many years in Marblehead, Massachusetts,
she died in 2001 at the age of ninety-two.

She wrote *The True Story of Saint Nicholas* in 1964
after hearing other parents say that Christmas was
too commercial and that Santa Claus should have
no part in it. Already a holiday tradition in many
families, it is being published once again so that
families might continue to read it together.

# ABOUT THE ILLUSTRATOR

Elizabeth Durham Goodhue grew up in Richmond, Virginia, and graduated from Sweet Briar College in 1939. She lived most of her adult life in Marblehead, Massachusetts, where she raised her two children and was active in community service. She died in 1973 at the age of fifty-five.

The only book Mrs. Goodhue ever illustrated, *The True Story of Saint Nicholas* is dedicated to her memory.

This edition of
THE TRUE STORY *of*
SAINT NICHOLAS
*was designed and typeset by*
*James F. Brisson*
*and published by*
*Alan C. Hood & Co., Inc.*
*in the year of our Lord*
*2006*